Gallery Books
Editor: Peter Fallon

ON BALLYCASTLE BEACH

Medbh McGuckian

ON BALLYCASTLE BEACH

Revised edition

Gallery Books

On Ballycastle Beach
is first published
simultaneously in paperback
and in a clothbound edition
on 30 March 1995.

The Gallery Press
Loughcrew
Oldcastle
County Meath
Ireland

ISBN 1 85235 157 8 (*paperback*)
     1 85235 158 6 (*clothbound*)

The Gallery Press receives financial assistance from An Chomhairle
Ealaíon / The Arts Council, Ireland, and acknowledges also the assis-
tance of The Arts Council of Northern Ireland in the publication of
this book.

Contents

for my aunts and uncles

What Does 'Early' Mean?

Happy house across the road,
My eighteen-inch deep study of you
Is like a chair carried out into the garden
And back again because the grass is wet.

Yet I think winter has ended
Privately in you, and lies in half-sleep,
Or her last sleep, at the foot
Of one of your mirrors — hence
The spring-day smile with which
You smarten up your mouth
Into a retina of new roofs, new thoughts.

None of my doors has slammed
Like that. Every sentence is the same
Old workshop sentence, ending
Rightly or wrongly in the ruins
Of an evening spent in puzzling
Over the meaning of six o'clock or seven:

Or why the house across the road
Has such a moist-day sort of name,
Evoking ships and their wind-blown ways.

Staying in a Better Hotel

Spring seemed to hold more weather
Than elsewhere; it was full of medicine,
A warning device whose tight flowers
I liked to watch, not breaking time,
But gathering in their least softness
The future saying 'soon' to the present.

From my hair I understood,
Like a house under construction,
How used I was to being kept alive:
A house so perfect all the doors
Grew smaller at the top, and
The windows were addressing the past.

Apple Flesh

The room getting lighter and darker
Is a kind of travel also.
No dream could find its way in here,
Up the now weak stairs,
Where my body tasted like apple flesh
The day and night of fifteen countries,
Or we sat about, unsmiling,
In a long, twisting sunset of 1910.

The thought of snow
Clutched my face like a train
Ducking clouds. I remembered
White pictures of birds and sun-healed
Water — birds that had lost
Their ability to shiver
And died in the brainwashed sea.

Rock pulled away from rock
Till the sea went out of its mind;
And my road in a sudden triangle
Warned how the dreamer is in danger
When his dream begins, like that,
With the weather.

My Brown Guest

Beyond all nervousness I loved
That ageing athlete, the hurricane,
Who left his screams behind him like a scarf.
The rose of sleep contaminated me,
Giving off scent in clouds — it had not yet learned
How to arrange the fullness
Of its hundred leaves. I brushed
His faults away, as in my mind I threw away
The truthfulness of the room — it was like
Trying to shovel away the sky, or the smell
Of snow, as meaningless and recognizable
As that of roses.

I sat where I could watch his hundred faces,
Nearly always half in mourning
For someone else whose house appeared
To be held in place by music —
(Though she heard, I believe, something different).
If at last I began to sense as ephemeral
What had already outlived most of the trees
It must have been the moon in her contraction
Bringing everything within reach, forcing
That window into a naked and murmuring triangle.

My low tide absorbed like a pencil-box
The ripple or the droop in my one small landing:
Remoteness swelled like the river's art in me,
Which keeps its people lightning-shaped,
However dark the night.

Sleep School

A wave stretching up so high,
Even I, Pomona, at the shore,
Goddess of gardens, felt the wash!
But only knew its *position* when
It started talking.

Sea-eyes, you said to me,
How well they haven't looked after
You! As though you could broaden
My maisonette with Elizabethan wings
In under half the time it takes to drown.

The water-clothing pulled back,
Showing its grass-grown roads, crying out
For more of my new-pressed wine;
But faintly, and unheard, like the webs
And stairs traced in my blue leather guest-book.

Because of the cloud, the sun moved
(Sleep watched him carefully) into
His next sky, where the sea matched
The pale brick colour of someone's having skated
All the scratches inside to the face.

A Conversation Set to Flowers

That fine china we conceived in spring
And lost in summer has blown the final crumbs
Out of the book I was reading; though one
Is still bending over prams, an ice-blue peak
Over the frills of houses.

The dress of ecru lace you bought me
At the February sales is still all heart.
I cup my hands, thin as a window-pane
Unevenly blown, as if to hold
Some liquid in my palm, and the rings
Slide up and down.

In my birth-dreams light falls in pleats
Or steps, the room after those terrible attacks
Is a white forest, scented with sea,
And we both change into apples, my breasts
And knees into apples, though you
Are more apple than they could possibly be.

But what the snow said, long ago,
To the grey north door and the short day,
Breaks through like the multi-coloured
Sunrise round a stamp on a letter.
A hill-wind blows at the book's edges
To open a page.

Sea or Sky?

Small doses, effleurage will do,
Because I never garden. Wednesday comes
Out of the rim of bones with a port-wine
Stain on its face, a day of possible
Excitements, no sky, yet you know immediately
The colour it should be. I play it down,
The agitated sky of my choice; I assume
That echo of light over there is the sun
Improperly burning. In a sea of like mood
A wave is trying to break, to give a reason
For water striking something else, and the grey
Below the wave is a darker version
Of the moisture-laden sky I should be working in.
(Not the clear water of your sleep where you
Seem lighter, and the garden's voice has gone inside.)

The athletic anatomy of waves, in their
Reflectiveness, rebirth, means my new, especially
Dense breasts can be touched, can be
Uplifted from the island of burned skin
Where my heart used to be, now I'm
Seeing eyes that, sea or sky, have seen you.

Gráinne's Sleep Song

The day that I got up to was not right.
It was hostile; it wanted to be alone
Like a novel rough to the touch. The house
Hadn't had enough sleep either
And in drudgery still heard the sound of kisses
Pursuing her. But 'That's how you should look,'
You said, as I put on my pre-war squirrel
Jacket. 'Not always in sports shoes.'
(Always in the very tempest of health,
Always waiting for the incomparable summer,
The demented autumn.) Like a porch in winter,
Blue, cold and affectionate, I stepped
With you for a moment out of my
Uncompleted story, something sterile
I contracted fourteen years ago on the beach,
Entitled 'Wild Without Love'. And stopping
In the entrance of strange houses, sudden
Downpours, I began to read, instead of
Letters never answered, well, salads
And love-walks. With a stone from the crop
Of my dark red, seven-by-nine, writing
Pad, I carved some verses I forget from
'Where Claribel Low Lieth', and beneath,
Both our initials in full.

Minus 18 Street

I never loved you more
Than when I let you sleep another hour,
As if you intended to make such a gate of time
Your home. Speechless as night animals,
The breeze and I breakfasted
With the pure desire of speech; but let
Each petal of your dream have its chance,
The many little shawls that covered you.

I never envied your child's face
Its motherless cheekbones or sensed in them
The approach of illness — how you were being
Half-killed on a seashore, or falling
From a ladder where you knelt to watch
The quartering of the moon. (You would never
Swim to the top of the rain that bathed
The mute world of her body.)

Sleep for you is a trick
Of the frost, a light green room in a French house,
Giving no trouble till spring.
The wedding-boots of the wind
Blow footsteps behind me.
I count each season for the sign
Of wasted children.

Sky of blue water, blue-water sky,
I sleep with the dubious kiss
Of my sky-blue portfolio.
Under or over the wind,
In soft and independent clothes,
I begin each dawn-coloured picture
Deep in your snow.

Not Pleasing Mama

If rain begins as snow, then the weather
Has slipped down as between walls, is not
To be trusted any more
Than any other magic.

Is an embayed window this hint of spring
Or a well-rounded outpour we collectively
Fall in love with?
Then I would ship the children off

Like the stone-coloured shirt I wear
By habit, with its sleeves closed
At the wrists, one of whose ambitions
It is to rustle,

Leaning back in the pillows *à la belle étoile*.
Autumn is a word that still draws pain,
Like a clown whose clothing
Got brighter and brighter

Or a widow smiling knowingly
At her dress becoming light above,
And dark below, a cloud
Having second thoughts.

Though all claims to next year's inflorescences —
For you are not a sleep of avoidance —
I secretly put out an apple on the pavement
To test you, growing colder and colder.

Ylang-Ylang

Her skin, though there were areas of death,
Was bright compared with the darkness
Working through it. When she wore black,
That rescued it, those regions were rested
Like a town at lighting-up time. In a heart-
Casket flickered her heartless 'jeune fille'
Perfume. I was compelled by her sunburnt,
Unripe story and her still-schoolgirl hand.

My life, sighed the grass-coloured,
Brandy-inspired carafe, is like a rug
That used to be a leopard, beckoning
To something pink. Yes, I replied, I have
A golf-coat almost as characterless,
Where all is leaf. We began moving over
Each other in the gentlest act of colour,
Not as far as the one-sided shape of red,

But out of that seriousness, out of the stout
Ruled notebook. She would stream in, her
Sculptor's blouse disturbed so by the violence
Of yellow. I would have to thank the light
For warning me of her approach. Not I,
But the weakened blue of my skirt
Wanted the thrown-together change, from vetiver
To last night's ylang-ylang, and back again.

Mazurka

Not only her mouth but her cry is left
Of 'Say it, say it, it isn't too early!
It isn't *like* a blow, it's a secret.'
(When they wait in that way, curtains
Of snow, curtains of leaves, she
Would go through the same snow again
For the same shoulders.)

In the deepest copper of a dream, perhaps,
A newly-understood poem will melt
And be hard again. Like dresses that go nowhere,
How they whiten at the anywhere
Kiss of a public place!
Indeed at this very hour, it is darkest
Especially for them
In that half-underground room where the
Just-above-ground chairs suck you down
To the last poem being aired on the last rug
By the very last fireplace.

On a russet bed he slept,
His lion-coloured hair curling away
From his shoulders like his wide-ranging
Blood; and his opened arms spread
Like the wings of a book, breaking into
A mazurka. That was the whole gist
Of his life, the burning velvet of encounters
Where the day starts flying the first
Of such years, and the mattress-striped
Front hallway was his sled, like a little
Blood-like drop, into the sea of tomorrow.

We, however, who dream of the first
And only sea, with our inland hair,
We dream in the speech
Of an apple left on a silver plate
Which measures the heat of blood;
And she was supposed to turn up
As it were in the threefold whiteness,
Or sevenfold longing of his dream,
As a blue shadow, the importance being
Less her than her little spark of *sea*.

If he were to go back over his dream again,
Past the white unpainted table, with the mirror
Where her soul was, with the notebook
Where her face was — would he even half
Detach himself from every bit of blue,
Pouring out about how high he comes up
On his father, marking his growth on a door?
(That white dress blowing,
That was love, that was snow.)

Blue Sky Rain

I thought I had broken tomorrow,
Tidying her away like that, like
Black satin clothes, or two women
In a step-liaison. My ultra-fervent
'Always' was a vague, deep coma,
Impassable for flowers, wherein
Less than half the days had any blue.
And though we lived then in a pink and white
Seaside house with green shutters (really
A kind of church, built out of old ships),
Nothing tinted the loneliness leading down
Continuously to the body-coloured beach.

Breast-shells, fairer than wheat, my second
Nature spied on there, and stole as from
A weather-sequence. Once, a small-bodied
Shadow asked me what I painted :—
It was her own superb, sienna eyes,
The long eyes of a child of the North,
With their woodland light. The stone-blue
Hours rumoured by, some blue sky rain
Exploited her still living hair like odd
Scraps of after-pains. It took me
Three whole days to get her little square hands
Exactly the same snow colour as the clouds.

Querencia

Her hands come awake from the apple-green shutters
Of sleep. She clasps the end of her leather belt tightly,
As if she can no longer speak for herself or only
With telephone distortions, the meaning of a row
Of black spinal buttons between sender and receiver.

Now here is her favourite cup with its matching plate
And a letter so young, something inside her feels
Just like the lines and better than sleep.
As she walks to the window, she smooths out her girlhood
Into a shadow of body-colour.

It is strange, how his eyelids close from below,
How love blows her hair to the right, his first beard
To the left. A face in a photograph destroyed
Since childhood catches her by the gate-legged
Oak table — the chance-seen face like a cold moonstone
In the window's sixteen panes.

She remembers his having to throw stones in the water
To break his dream — and how the river returned them —
Or seated at the stone table under the yew, explaining
His need for streets.

At which the birds and vine bed-hangings complain, we have
Been taken in too many times by leaves against the window:
A window should be a wide-eaved colour beyond anything.

Death of a Ceiling

The sounds that shapes make in the air,
The shapes that sounds make, matter
Whenever a stone or pocket-knife
Is rocketed through water.

So lightning arranges the logarithms
Of ferns, equates the radius
Of the moon to the number of breaths
We draw in an hour.

The flowers of the past
Closed with an endless flickering.
Even after the outer petals
Lit up like a line of lamps,
The kiss of the other day
Was the one they were most against.

And yet it could only have lain
In wait, like the decorous seeds
Of the sunflower — each spiral brighter
By four more than that within.

I thought so darkly down
My left arm of a voice-coloured
Garden he has blundered upon,
Once or twice, I got the dead
Lavender away. How long

Will that garden be a garden?
As long as the picture spoken
By the window makes no claim
To be any closer a branch-pattern
Than glass should be.

And the rooms that were all paragraphed
By either a step up or down,
I should have entirely papered
With used postage-stamps:

Their leaf-mould letting out the house
Into a red linen, quaker brown,
Brew of so many fruits between
The element that suits him, and mine.

First Letters from a Steamer

The green of old leaves was my breasts'
Remembered pleasure: what season are you,
Spring woman, winter woman? Four
Perfect springs make this season
A kind of agony, the sea turns on
Another light, as other friends
Have done in other ways.

Long before a flower opens
The number of its petals is established,
And if I took some sunlight
When I felt the foggy days, it was
A red coat I'm still a little afraid of,
Like realizing one was very hungry,
Or very thirsty, eating only what the soil yields.

A broken vase I loved
Had four small pieces out of the rim
And three were saved — I covered it
With clear cement and painted a half-inch
Carnation over the seams. The handle
Of the chipped cup has been shaved off
Into a perfect sugar-bowl.

Where my Irish life begins there is
A tennis court that became a hayfield
And never was remade.
You smooth the back of one hand
With the other like frozen blossoms,
Fruit that won't go into your jars.
But I would not have shortened the rain

Since the way he takes his applause
Is through the warm sun on our plates,
And the paper in his piano
Gives the sounds of his Ds and Bs and As
The colours of being buried in the earth:
Brown over my shoulders, red over my feet,
Tonight I'll use up a little blue on you.

Blue Vase

My overblouse is a garment made
For rest, work, movement. I permit
On my body only that which glides,
The roving ache of all shared things —
Love, rest, and dreams.

My house is a small blue vase,
As difficult to give you as a present
From a trousseau or layette, being
Held too tightly by my own
Determined touch:

Determined to steady your heart,
As a painting that gathers up
The light of some astonishing hair,
The rare dimming of a ship
Early in the voyage.

Not losing his temper will come out
In one man's paintings of forty
Of his dreams, his stair-step children,
As if he had studied all the dreams
Dreamt in one night

With the same fierceness with which
We treat a fever. In the dream
That preceded the poem, I was standing
Outside a house that had your face;
From opposite ends

Re-chose you in my dream-speech,
Without telling you or anyone what it meant:
To be the insouciance of the room,
Interrupted, re-created — to be the innocence
You have just learned to say.

The Blue She Brings with Her

for Teresa

November — like a man taking all
His shirts, and all his ties, little by little —
Enters a million leaves, and that
Lion-coloured house-number, the sun,
Into his diary; with a rounded symbol —
Nothing — to remind himself of callow apples,
Dropping with a sense of rehearsal in June
As if their thought were being done by others.

The mirror bites into me as cloud into
The river-lip of a three-cornered lake
That when the moon is new is shaped
Like the moon. With a sudden crash
My log falls to ashes, a wood of winter
Colours I have never seen — blood-kissed,
The gold-patterned dishes
Show themselves for a moment like wild creatures.

While any smoke that might be going loose
The hot room gathers like a mountain
Putting out a mist, and not the kind that clears.
Something you add about mountains makes
My mouth water like a half-lifted cloud
I would choose, if I could, to restrain
As a stone keeps its memories.

Your eyes change colour as you move
And will not go into words. Their swanless
Sky-curve holds like a conscious star
A promise from the wind about the blue
She brings with her. If beauty lives
By escaping and leaves a mark, your wrist
Will have the mark of my fingers in the morning.

Four O'Clock, Summer Street

As a child cries, all over, I kept insisting
On robin's egg blue tiles about the fireplace,
Which gives a room a kind of flying-heartedness.

Only that tiny slice of the house absorbed
My perfume — like a kiss sliding off into
A three-sided mirror — like a red-brown girl

In cuffless trousers we add to ourselves by looking.
She had the boy-girl body of a flower,
Moving once and for all past the hermetic front door.

I knew she was drinking blue and it had dried
In her; she carried it wide awake in herself
Ever after, and its music blew that other look

To bits. If what she hunted for could fit my eyes,
I would shine in the window of her blood like wine,
Or perfume, or till nothing was left of me but listening.

Lighthouse with Dead Leaves

I was dissecting the brain of a child when I cut
My less than agile finger.
(One should keep aside
A pair of loose, black, cotton gloves
For shaking hands with children.)

When the blood ran to its sleeping places
What dreams returned or were allowed to grow,
As if a ship that opened her planks
To the carpentry of the sea
Became a thinking fog in which
All wounds began to glow,
And lighthouses sprang to mind?

Dead leaves and water, maybe he recollected
Walking two miles in the rain to wave goodbye
And walking into the sky.
Like an outswollen shoe
That fits inside another or
Swans that but appear
To be dancing to music,
So his love-nest is creeping over me,
Is keeping me amused
Till I am three girls or the same girl
Leading him, a figure no longer
Dreamt about, nor dreaming,
But partner to me like a ruptured seed.

I have locked my bedroom door from the inside
And do not expect it to be mutilated.
My garb is chosen for a dry journey;
Sleep will be a line of trees searching for this stable
I would have left to rot if I'd been able.

Little House, Big House

In a day or two the chairs will fall to pieces.
Those who were once lovers need the minimum
Of furniture, half-people, each with his separate sky.

Christmas peered through the escallonia hedge
And passed almost unnoticed, except the stamps
Had squirrels on them. Why should I take
My apron off for a wineless dinner? My things
Are too grey; like a tree I deepen shadows
With my brown autumn raincoat.

On the ground floor, one room opens into another,
And a small Matisse in the inglenook
Without its wood fire is stroked by light
From north and south. That started all the feelings
That had slept till then. I came out
From behind the teapot to find myself
Cooled by a new arrangement of doorways
And choosing a spiced bun from a china shell.

A shawl no whiter than my white skin
Made me a dust-jacket. I overwatered
The Michaelmas daisies thinking about
The claw-like bedroom door-handles along
The minstrel's gallery. And the house like me
Was tangled with the emotion of cut flowers —

So different from an ordinary going-away —
That I could hardly keep my hand
From phoning you, impromptu. Since our blood
Is always older than we will ever be,
I should like to lie in Tarusa under matted winter grass,
Where the strawberries are redder than anywhere else.

Coleridge

for Michael Longley

In a dream he fled the house
At the Y of three streets
To where a roof of bloom lay hidden
In the affectation of the night,
As only the future can be. Very tightly,
Like a seam, she nursed the gradients
Of his poetry in her head;
She got used to its movements like
A glass bell being struck
With a padded hammer.
It was her own fogs and fragrances
That crawled into the verse, the
Impression of cold braids finding
Radiant escape, as if each stanza
Were a lamp that burned between
Their beds, or they were writing
The poems in a place of birth together.
Quietened by drought, his breathing
Just became audible where a little
Silk-mill emptied impetuously into it
Some word that grew with him as a child's
Arm or leg. If she stood up (easy,
Easy) it was the warmth that finally
Leaves the golden pippin for the
Cider, or the sunshine of fallen trees.

To a Cuckoo at Coolanlough

for Peter Fallon

Driving the perfect length of Ireland,
Like a worn fold in a newspaper,
All my deep, country feelings
Wished I could have hypnotized myself
Into going back for the cherry-market
At Borris-in-Ossory.

But all I could think of was the fountain
Where Shelley wrote his 'Ode to the West Wind'
Nesting like a train-fever or combing jacket
Over the town.

A child will only sleep so long, and I wonder
If he is an artist, or have the six
Muscles around his eye forgotten colour,
And look it up, that Saturn-red, wild smudging,
In a dream-book?

And I wonder, after the three-minute
News, if you remember
The bits of road that I do?

Frost in Beaconsfield

A voice beyond a door that cuts off
The words was my coverless book to you,
Myself the price of it. You took your pen,
Like summer sending out spokes of night,
Or wooden tongue-blades, summer after
Summer in the same place, and manufactured
A forest of half-friends, from out-and-out
Enemies, in the criss-cross window-pane.

That picture had to live with you, the field-size
Soul of a scientist flying into rain
That has accidentally kissed a too-heavy
Blossom, asking where does the day begin,
At the puritan dawn of the bosom?

So much is known by the dredging winds
That are apt to sweep into bed with any
Cold or tired body. Early morning
Walked with all her loops and ties
In her black worsted stockings
Through the frost which was a recent thing.
The clouds turned their sides towards
The usefulness of blue, all of them
Thought out by the last sounds of dark.

Balakhana

A town will never draw your mind to it
Like a place where you have camped.
You will remember the very curve
Of your wagon-track in the grass
Where the ring swayed and was broken, almost,
As if someone had cried a message to you,
In one word, once, and would not repeat it.

Compare the most metallic of sounds,
The sound of elevators at night, or a car
Stopping outside, a plane throwing herself
Forward into space. The door I found
So difficult to close let in my first
European feeling which now blows about,
A cream-coloured blossom, with a blue vigour.

And if it were spring I would have sold
My leather jacket back to the short rains,
And folded, or unfolded, slowly
Through all the burning hours of the day,
As if a giant upright cloud had been tied to me.

That flap of earth leaned against the sun
As women lean their faces to the wall
Giving birth. Its mountains stretched
And spread and strangely took shape
From the smells that ran along them,
Their deeply responsible pauses and heights
Striking sphere after sphere of sparks.

Inside me everything was blurred
Like tea with smoked milk, the stone
In the fruit, the meaning, the child
That left me no ground. As I stood
In thought by a window, I saw the glass-
Clear sky above my head like solid
Floorwork, become a sword half

Out of its scabbard, and suddenly
Filled like a glass with wine.
As if from its high site it too had drunk in
More than one stormy sunset, and more
Than blood.

Things of the same kind are separated
Only by time — I prayed the moon,
Meant only for the moment,
Would have it in him
To go on as beautifully as he had begun.

For a Young Matron

New dust in the heat-collecting
Top floor. Her eyes
Add a brown look
With a bleached oak pencil.

Approaching all colours
From their peaks,
We try to imagine each sentence
In a crosstown light.

Why not forget this word,
He asks. It's edgeless,
Echoless, it is stretched so,
You cannot become its passenger.

An aeroplane unlike
A womb claims its space
And takes it with it.
It says, Once it wasn't like this.

But wood grows
Like the heart worn thin
Within us, or the original
Spirit of October.

Girls in the Plural

The shadow of a summer tightly folded
Fitted without violence over the shoulders
And breasts of separating roses, though no one
Was passing the window.

I let it lie there a twelvemonth,
A wistful, clinging letter,
Reflected in my mirror, listening to my clock,
As one who had never given herself to him,
But found herself with child, and frittered
Away the thoughtless wind that grew in her
Like some deflowered ghost.

Lost days, while far away
Cells were ordered otherwise.

My closed eyes had just made up
That simile about his eyes awakening,
The colour of their fear, a promise halved.
I had ransacked the world for stained
Wings of the same possessive fabric,
But none of my removals
Was in any sense a flight —

More the invention of a new caress
Wearing off like pain unmixed
With the round poems, the edged tools,
Pressing like a damaged cloud against the doors.

Elsewhere, he
Breathed in the air that belonged to me.

Harem Trousers

for Nuala Ní Dhomhnaill

Asleep on the coast I dream of the city.
A poem dreams of being written
Without the pronoun 'I'.

The river bends lovingly
Towards this one, or that one, or a third.
The staircase resumes its never-mentioned
Ladder shape, as anything
That is being hurt overflows its innocence.

It straightens, stands, it walks
Timid and incongruous
Through roadblocks and breadlines.
It holds the hundred and first word
In its fingers and tears it apart,

So the openness within the sound
Is forced to break, dislodging
Its already dove-grey music.
An extreme and simple feeling
Of 'What if I do enter?' —

As I run to fetch water
In my mouse-coloured sweater,
Unkempt, hysterical, from
The river that lives outside me,
The bed whose dishevelment
Does not enchant me.

Your room speaks of morning,
A stem, a verb, a rhyme,
From whose involuntary window one
May be expelled at any time,
As trying to control a dream
Puts the just-completed light to rest.

A Dream in Three Colours

I am velvet stroked the wrong way.
The interval between my poems is like
The light between seasons, or the darkness
A mountain is filled with.

The point when I sleep is not known
By me, and words cannot carry me
Over it — it is heard only like a kiss
That flows and is not torn out.

Every hour the voices of nouns
Wind me up from their scattered rooms,
Where they sit for years, unable to meet,
Like pearls that have lost their clasp,

Or boards snapped by sea-water
That slither towards a shore.
Far more raw than the spring night
Which shook you out of its sleeve,

Your first winter sheds for you
Its strongest blue, its deepest white,
Its reddest silk lapel you can let go
Or hold, whichever you love best.

The Time Before You

for Paul Muldoon

The secret of movement
Is not the secret itself
But the movement
Of there being a secret.

For example, the movement
Of an accordion which closes
On one side and opens
On the other.

Or your folding one arm
Against your pushing body
At the turn towards waking
Which is the full length

Of your dream. When
You look at me as a man
May look, it is like a break
Of real sky where one branch

Crosses its fellow, a brown leaf
Taking September into
A brown stone, or green
Under green, grass below trees.

You ask the difference
Between a green shadow
And a brown one? Here
Is a green answer.

I can only say
I feel that green shadow,
That short, morning shadow,
Through and through me,

With a sense of hair in a coil
Recoiling from the fingers
That held it, smoothing
Its darkness till it would seem

Like whatever it is furthest
From, one of those blonde
Napes velvety as leaves
With the tip pointed towards you.

By now you will have painted
The first of the sea fresh-staring
Yellow and changed its name.
So that now I always hear

The sea in the wind, though
I like a wind in which
You hear the rain, however moist
With breath its mask may be.

And after last night's rain
I actually dreamed of you,
Falling asleep for that
Wild purpose, seeing

Your face through the floor
As all the light left
On the flat of a hand.
I wish they could hear

That we lived in one room
And littered a new poetry
Long after both doors, up-
And downstairs, shut.

To the Oak-Leaf Camps

for Irina Ratushinskaya

Both of us lie in the dark to compose
Verses as we were taught. I think of them
As a child you know will be born dead
At three minutes to ten, and put my hands
Behind my back à la papa, persuaded
That the last pain of the second stage
Is no worse than the one before the last.

To know that must be to crush
A small bird to death every morning
For fifty-two days, and hold its fresh
Blood in the mouth, red of red,
As a book read robs you of the fever
You had when you were writing it.

Your sky is as close to me
As some particular garment — a cloud
There changes into another set of arms
In the time required to dress, undress.
Someone has mixed eau-de-cologne
With sugar so my heart of sixteen
Is slowed down to a hundred.

And though I draw back
More than half-a-step,
Nothing in the world but the sight
Of a map makes me subtract
Our shared portmanteau name
From my few yards of pavement,
Misshapen even to all-year-round birds.

Scenes from a Brothel

Daughters of different mothers may have
The same eyes, but not the same look
In their eyes, for only stone goes well with water.

One has lips so virginal, they seem to be edged
With snow, the discoloured whiteness waiting
Within ourselves.
Her teeth are pressed like seeds
Against one another, all her bones are armour,
And anything one says reaches the scroll
Of her body slowly, her madonna
Parting, her milk-fed hands.

I would prefer to be kissed by other
Grown-up lips, but her younger sister
Speaks with the rapid beating of fish
Breathing out of water.
Her face glitters, becoming blurred
Like blondes in warm countries.
She stands as though interrupted
In a swift movement, or kissing in flight,
Her gown a whirlwind of silk flowers
Open to bursting-point.

Any colour lasts a second, three or four
Minutes at most — and can never be repeated.
So few words for so many colours.
This blue, this blue, an enfeebled red,
The child of old parents.
Though it is immutable, it has no more lustre
Than the moon in its first quarter
Or the wall above the coat-stand.

I wish her room were a square bed
With the sheets gushing up like a beautiful
Expanse of water. The mirror doubles distances
So the garden is a cascade of paths.
How cold the sea must be,
To make all faces the same!

She lets her arm rest, like the tulip's turn,
On the wheat of her voice. She splashes
The much-caressed sky till its distress
Is lighted from the other side.
The silk cracks at its blue corners
As if her bones were the weight and shape of birds'.

The Bird Auction

Trees, heavier and darker:
Their voices carry stones.
With lips well-reddened
They give a black kiss.

Through the blood-coloured glass
On the women's side of the chapel,
Each stain reaches the eye
Unweathertight, by itself.

One opens for a moment
An umbrella made of bright
Yellow cotton, lined with green,
That somehow the sun never got into,

Turning it before the fire
Like a girl in a satin dinner dress.
In little sitting-out places
Between palms and pots of flowers,

They are hanging sheets over doorways,
Keeping them wet with chloride of lime.
And one arrangement of matter
Is the castle where O'Neill slept

His last night in Ireland, the other
Is the view at which Byron
Never tired of gazing. They
Are auctioning his bed,

His too rich words, the rent table,
The chest that hides an altar, any
Horse of value, so many
Fragrant and delicious souvenirs

As I sat forgetting it.

On Not Being Listened To

You respect the flowers when they pass
Out of your hands. You hold to words
Because they have been said. You will
Take two days from a fine little chain
And hold them against me, every separate
Thing remembered like the last day
Of the year, mottling it over with
Your feet as a child might snow.

The rain gives the window or its equivalent
An example of pouring on, the sun
In his storing-journeys imagines the early
Farness of nine-in-the-morning. One
Quarter of the staircase asks to know
What you have written, within the summer's
Hearing, on the closed throat of the envelope.

Through the Round Window

In my desk I have a ring
With many smaller rings attached;
When I lie in the faithful bed
I become a brooch in the shape of an anchor.
Tell the white canoe, without an owner,
That the serious breezes have long been over —
It is half a winter since he sought me
Like a taste where glens run inland
Where the white sailing-boat injured itself
Three years ago. That same night
Piano lessons were going on somewhere,
Beyond the courtyard a child playing Brahms
Hurt his mouth on the music-rack,
And perfume struck me like a sudden cry.

They say that music has to be heard
In the dark; but when I have no news of sleep
I feel the room being torn to pieces, till no black
Is connected to any other black, my yellow
Pencil, my green table, can never be lit again.
Each poem in my alchemist's cupboard
That was an act of astonishment has a life
Of roughly six weeks, less than half a winter
Even in the child's sense of a week. The tray
Clinks silver in the stage before coldness;
As if I were ill a card comes, decorated
With roses. I fold it with my ring-finger.

The Sky Marshal

At the stress-points of a shell
Grows a little grey pearl
The shape of a child's tooth
Aged sixteen months and asleep.

Days of dark beard,
Like a rain of earth or a scalp
Of turf, push into the stomach
Powder that remains of it.

The past is large and last
Year's calendar with the picture
Of the Teardrop of Ireland, Paddy's Milestone,
Sticks like a fever to the wall.

If happiness occurs, it is more likely
In winter, in a field
Of winter wheat under
Concentrated snow, and not

When leaves are half drawn-in
Because of extreme heat,
Or in sun-dried rooms where it is
Unspeakably cold,

Each person occupying the half
Of a sofa, each road seeming
To bring a wind with it
Like the empty veins of a leaf —

As fuchsia was brought here
In 1823 from South America —
As nature withdraws her claim
On the senses of five or six

Leaf-sockets — and as my pen
Beginning with a walk must
End with a meeting. So you know
I've been doing nothing

But ask you questions since the eighth
Of this month: are you unfaithful?
Are you dead? Under what trees
Will you be happy in fifteen years

With your children? Three out of their
Six eyes are blue, and I am brown
Of hair. But just below
The much-kissed breast-bone

Of your body where I broke
The poem open, pressing my lips
In a tighter, sadder way,
A long spring cloud

Crushed its starry shirt
Like the marrow of a
Monday-night husband
Through my ill-closed door.

Yeastlight

You speak like the rain, as if you were the weather.
I can almost see the passage of wine through your throat
As you swallow, its colour seems to be standing
Behind you, in the designer-blue air. When I found
In the very cup of the town those poems sewn
Into cushions, or pushed into saucepans or shoes,
I took the arm of someone I didn't know
Who turned over all my mattresses
And shook out every book.

I could not have imagined pearls had such warmth.
My house planned to catch the sun in all
Its rooms, in the shape of a fan, seemed no better
Than other houses; its clear note had gone out
And fallen in with the wind which sometimes
Sounds so much like rain, the passing
Of wise hands over shoulders, the frisking
Of clothing that remoulds you and restrains you,
Back into the narrow bed of a girl.

Still my dining-room, with its gold oak-leaf
Paper, has three long windows looking west
Upon a ligulate forest, and *famille rose*,
Famille verte, china for an up-with-the-kettle,
Round-with-the-car, man, if you could not bear
To have it going on one moment longer,
Doors with their fertile roar, their desert
Glances, closing from the inside, not the out-
Or to have it ever stopped.

Head of a Woman

The tendon of the day is strained,
The week is plunged into deep shadow
Lighter than the skin of my face.
This morning I joined my elbows
To hide my breasts, that single gesture
Has created a body for itself, the sun
In his dispersal of activity was unable
To shake out my close-laid hair, its
Heavy nocturnal concentration. It was
A face that grew under his hand,
His hand waits to give the movement
Completing my head. It was a face
To which a hand found its way
Out of another study, and settled
On my swollen lips like a bird
That understands the role of air perfectly.
I was seated, I gathered my limbs
Under me, to suppress my shadow,
To cool my light as if I were a park.
My kisses were insane because they
Burnt without refreshing; they were chains
That had prepared their answers. Now
It is four o'clock, the high tide
Belongs to him, the shock of his deep
Breathing moves me by reminiscences,
There are just enough words for a
New distribution of light. The
Preliminaries of night pass nervously
Across my cheeks, an owl on its arms
And in its hair, a world that sleeps
And becomes fertile, not leaving any fragment
Of itself unused. And still the dawn
Seeking the shared spirals of my mouth
Listens like a lost colour
And has not broken.

The Dream-Language of Fergus

1

Your tongue has spent the night
In its dim sack as the shape of your foot
In its cave. Not the rudiment
Of half a vanquished sound,
The excommunicated shadow of a name,
Has rumpled the sheets of your mouth.

2

So Latin sleeps, they say, in Russian speech,
So one river inserted into another
Becomes a leaping, glistening, splashed
And scattered alphabet
Jutting out from the voice,
Till what began as a dog's bark
Ends with bronze, what began
With honey ends with ice;
As if an aeroplane in full flight
Launched a second plane,
The sky is stabbed by their exits
And the mistaken meaning of each.

3

Conversation is as necessary
Among these familiar campus trees
As the apartness of torches;
And if I am a threader
Of double-stranded words, whose
Quando has grown into now,
No text can return the honey
In its path of light from a jar,
Only a seed-fund, a pendulum,
Pressing out the diasporic snow.

Woman with Blue-Ringed Bowl

for my mother

Like a curtain opening a glade in a children's bedroom,
Her fallen shawl unpins a brown and fallen breast.
If I was possessed of a pen that wrote in four colours,
I could patrol how differently each tree contains the sun.
Hold me in the light, she offers, turn me around,
Not the light controlled by a window, but the cool gold
Of turning leaves after their short career in the sky.

She is refolding the rind of the orange she has just eaten
And will drop it now on the grass that is virgin every year.
Are her eyes half-closed and her lips half-open, what with
Lack of sleep or struggling with the surprise of the word 'no'?
She has a flower-seller's walk, the sister of calm;
She has that quality of night I most care for,
Pressing years into days like a poet of night.

Though six vigorous soldiers have occupied her house,
She has cried out only once, and laughed without a wrinkle.
As wine comes stepping from stones, adding death to death,
A quarter of her blood shows like a scar at moments
Of excitement through her belted dress of dusky grey.
You would think it grey, but I think her dress
Is worthy of her mind, the semi-darkness
Of a poem composed after illness.

That evening, when I printed THE END in my black,
Floral, author's hand, on the blended orangey page,
I gave my youth to my mother, whose heart is not
Supposed to beat, even on the stairs, and said to the
Moroccan April, Stay the way you are.

A gust of wind, and colour flies to the door
That cannot be kept so narrow, my notebook lies
Useless as a womb on my knees. The blue ensnared
Is a careful, sad, a Marie-Louise blue,
And she has remained both woman and flaxen page.
But, when I saw the picture again, the sun had gone.

On Ballycastle Beach

for my father

If I found you wandering round the edge
Of a French-born sea, when children
Should be taken in by their parents,
I would read these words to you,
Like a ship coming in to harbour,
As meaningless and full of meaning
As the homeless flow of life
From room to homesick room.

The words and you would fall asleep,
Sheltering just beyond my reach
In a city that has vanished to regain
Its language. My words are traps
Through which you pick your way
From a damp March to an April date,
Or a mid-August misstep; until enough winter
Makes you throw your watch, the heartbeat
Of everyone present, out into the snow.

My forbidden squares and your small circles
Were a book that formed within you
In some pocket, so permanently distended,
That what does not face north, faces east.
Your hand, dark as a cedar lane by nature,
Grows more and more tired of the skidding light,
The hunched-up waves, and all the wet clothing,
Toys and treasures of a late summer house.

Even the Atlantic has begun its breakdown
Like a heavy mask thinned out scene after scene
In a more protected time — like one who has

Gradually, unnoticed, lengthened her pre-wedding
Dress. But, staring at the old escape and release
Of the water's speech, faithless to the end,
Your voice was the longest I heard in my mind,
Although I had forgotten there could be such light.